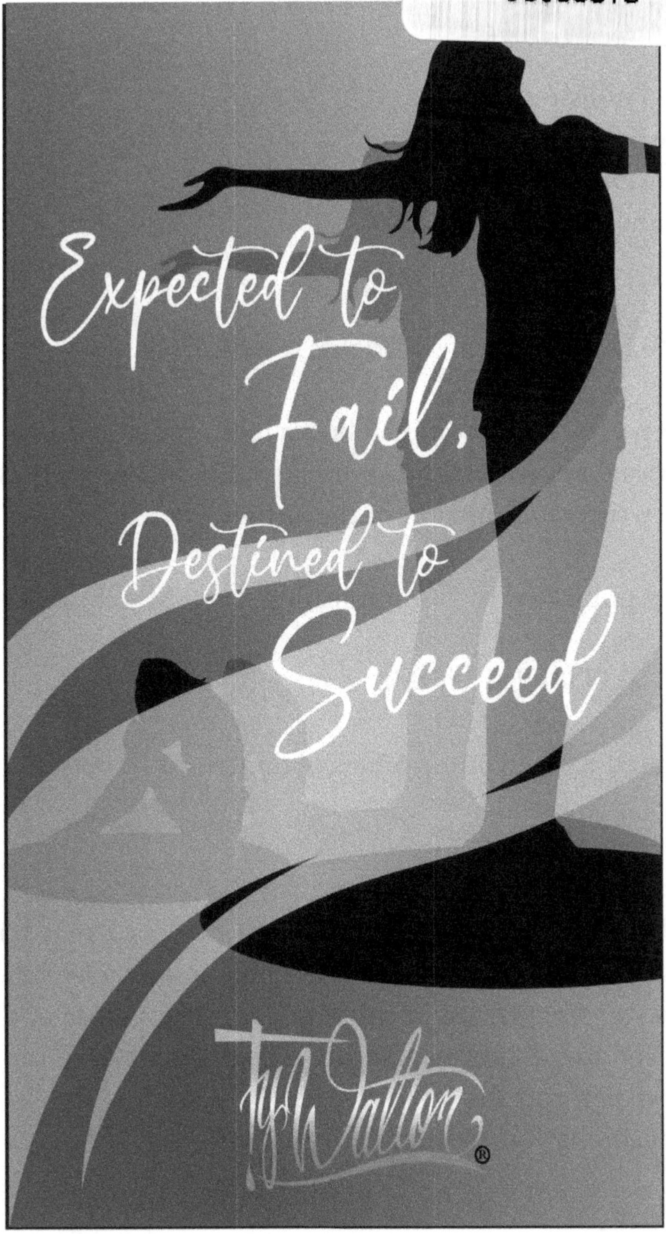
Expected to
Fail,
Destined to
Succeed
Ty Walton®

3G Publishing, Inc.
Loganville, Ga 30052
www.3gpublishinginc.com
Phone: 1-888-442-9637

©2021 Ty Walton. All rights reserved.

No part of this book may be reproduced, stored in a retrieval system, or transmitted by any means without the written permission of the author.

First published by 3G Publishing, Inc. March, 2021.

ISBN: 9781941247877

Printed in the United States of America

Because of the dynamic nature of the Internet, any web addresses or links contained in this book may have changed since publication and may no longer be valid. The views expressed in this work are solely those of the author and do not necessarily reflect the views of the publisher, and the publisher hereby disclaims any responsibility for them.

Contents

Foreword	5
Acknowledgements	9
Introduction	11
Chapter I Humble Beginnings	15
Chapter II Wanted But Unwanted	31
Chapter III The Expectation	41
Chapter IV Dates With Destiny	47
Chapter V Ready or Not	75
Chapter VI Destiny Displayed	97
Conclusion	107

Foreword

There is perhaps no worse feeling than the feeling that one has failed. Whether it is a test in school or failing a physical for a job, or failing the driver's license test, it has a way of deflating you and making you not want to try again. But one of my favorite sayings is "just because you fail doesn't make you a failure." It was said that Thomas Edison failed over 2000 times when trying to invent the light bulb. When asked how he felt after failing so many times, his response was, "I just found 2000 ways how not to do it." In this book, you are going to hear from a young lady who had every reason to give up. With so many things going against her, she could have easily quit and become a statistic. But she rose and became a mighty, anointed, vessel of God. I am sure you will be challenged, but most of all encouraged as you read this awesome book! I am glad to say that I was her pastor for many years and saw her grow in God and in life. She is a fighter, and a prayer warrior spiritually, an entrepreneur and wife and mother in the natural realm. One of the things I say so often is, "EV-

ERYONE HAS A STORY!" You are going to be greatly blessed as you hear Pastor Ty's story about how she was EXPECTED TO FAIL, BUT DESTINED TO WIN!!

-Pastor Kelvin Ransey
Pastor of The Spirit of Excellence Ministries and
Prelate of United in Christ

Over 25 years ago, I met a young lady who was broken, confused, and damaged, just to name a few of her seemingly many ails. She was expected to fail by her peers, and adults. But God. He changed the narrative of her life, for today she is successful. She was a diamond in the rough. A young woman with exceptional qualities and characteristics that could not be seen from the surface. But God called her, His daughter.

Ty's story is one of how when God calls you out, chooses you and calls you His son or daughter, you receive His favor. Ty is a worshipper, a praiser, and a prayer warrior. I know that there were many things and opportunities that she did not qualify for, but it makes a difference when God writes your resume. From broken to blessed and favored, from confused to consecrated for her Fathers work - damaged but destined to succeed. What a story!

Her story could be your story. People and society may count you out, but that is when you are exactly right for God to count you in. He did it for her, He can do it for you. So, I am confident that her story will bless your life as you take the time to read it.

~Joseph Hawkins

Acknowledgements

First to my Daddy! The only one I know! He is the Creator, the King, and simply a good, good Father that excessively loves me!

To the woman who did not have much to give, but she made it her life to give me Jesus – Mama, I love you girl!!

To the man who taught me how to fight in the spirit and convinced me he loves me - My husband!

To ALL my children, especially the ones God trusted me to birth-Debrico, Sheluv, and Daniel; for you I WAR!

To my grandchildren, for you I FIGHT!

To my divine sister and the one whom God sent to hold my hand- Natoria Kennell Foster.

To my best friend and the one that Daddy simply told me to "trust the connection" – Prophetess Asheena Simmons!

To my Apostolic mentor- Ramona Stevens-Donley!

To my natural Naomi - Mary L. Boyde!
And last, but certainly not least, the one who challenged me to leave my heart on paper - Owerri Marrasha Washington and the ones responsible for the finished product you are holding in your hands - 3G Publishing, Inc. Thank you seems so inadequate!!!

Introduction

As a child, my life was incredibly challenging. Growing up in the projects of Tupelo, MS one might ask the same question that was asked regarding Mary the mother of Jesus…"Can anything good come out of the projects on Green Street?" After years of continual process and many detours, the response to the question is certainly, something good can come out of the projects on Green Street!

This book will allow you to see a God-ordained success story that was birthed from a dysfunctional family, in a home where the older brother was forced to carry on the role of three absent fathers, and a single mother who worked multiple jobs to provide for her four children. Being the only girl of three brothers, I was forced to grow up at an incredibly young age to assist with the day-to-day mandates of a one parent family. This situation seemed exactly right for the enemy to speak a future of imminent failure over our lives.

The danger of not knowing who I was left space for the enemy to define me as I became the target and a victim of his plan of deceit. Surely, he felt his initial plan would be successful as he personified himself using my older brother's voice and the rejection of my biological father. The seemingly daily declaration that I would be "barefoot and pregnant by the time I was fifteen" played out just as declared by the enemy simply because I had not yet heard and understood the lessons of the power of words spoken over my life. If only I had heard and embraced Proverbs 18:21 that said, "Death and life are in the power of the tongue; and they that love it shall eat the fruit thereof (KJV)," sooner!

It was not until the damage was done and the enemies' words had been fulfilled in my life that I understood the demonic declarations that had been spoken over my life. Yes, certainly the enemy (not my older brother) EXPECTED ME TO FAIL, but God had already PRE-DESTINED ME TO SUCCEED. Even in the face of detours, the Lord had a plan, and he would watch over his word to come to pass in my life. (Jeremiah 1:12 AMP) Ultimately, the purpose of

God would not allow me to die where the enemy left me.

God has commissioned me to put my life on paper for that young girl, woman, boy, or man that the enemy has made some declarations over your life. The Lord has sent me to counter-attack those words declared over your life to tell you, "You were expected to fail, but before the foundations of the world, the Lord destined you to succeed!!" YES YOU!!!

Chapter I
Humble Beginnings

In the cool, fall month of November in 1978, an innocent, bald headed bundle of joy entered this world. At the time, I was the second child born to my single mother, out of wedlock. I would grow to know that my mother was a hard worker and would do whatever it took to provide for her two babies. Her drive to make sure my brother and I were cared for would lead her to work multiple jobs. In her diligence to provide for us, my brother and I would be kept by our grandparents until our grandfather died and later, the loss of the family home to a house fire.

It was about the age of four I can vividly remember the tragedy that would forever change our family dynamics. That would be the memories of our home that would be suddenly taken away from us due to a devastating house fire. On this cold night, my brother awakened to the house in the country already engulfed in flames and smoke. I can recall him running across the street to my aunt's house in a desperate plea for help. At the same time, my elderly grandmother was also trying to get out of the house. During the confusion, my brother realized that his baby sister was still in the house. He re-enters the house and through the desperate cries of, "I can't make it out" and the responses of, "get on your knees and come on out," he managed to make it out of the house with the both of us alive.

Not only did we lose our family home to a devastating fire, but we lost the only sense of stability known as children of a single parent. We lost the protection of our ability to enjoy life as children should. For me, I lost my sense of security. My grandmother was that protection that would allow me to maintain my childhood innocence without the early exposures of adulthood. She was the force that allowed me to take my time and enjoy the necessities of childhood. I was not ready for the days ahead which began a cycle of relentless instability for my family.

With my grandmother no longer in the home, life warranted that I learn to cook full meals by the age of seven and be responsible for managing the finances of our home by the time I was in middle school. One may ask what does this responsibility look like? This would mean forfeiting childhood to learn prematurely, what adulthood really is. It meant meal preparation instead of enjoying dolls and outdoors. As a matter of fact, I never owned a doll as a child and certainly do not remember playing with dolls which is a known developmental milestone of a female child. I learned early how to navigate the grocery store for foods that would feed the family. Grocery store trips were not an opportunity to ask for what you want, but rather an engaged moment with my mother, learning the ropes of feeding multiple mouths for a month with an allotted amount of government funds. I would become skilled at adding ingredients without measuring cups to appease the varying taste buds that would sit at the table. I know this seems like a lot, but hopefully you understand this task was far outside the scope of responsibilities for an innocent child who should be looking forward to school the next day. The financial responsibilities mandated this middle school child understand what it meant to "make do" and decide what monthly bills could be paid with the allotted monies from a mother working multiple jobs.

There were times we would be out of essential ingredients like flour, meal, or sugar. My mom did not believe in us borrowing what we may or may not be able to pay back. The options were make do or do without. I have had cornbread without eggs, Kool-Aid with less than required amounts of sugar, and meat only because there were no ingredients for the cornbread. I know what it is like to take a bath in cold water because there was no electricity. I learned to be grateful for the days we had electricity so we could warm ourselves by the heat of the oven. I know what it is to make sure the necessary things are completed in the daylight, because the lights would not be back on until next pay day which could be two to three days away. Financially, I learned why Mama made sure she met the deadline to sign us up for the Angel Tree every year. Without this community resource, there would be no Christmas as the world defines. I learned to be incredibly grateful for the second-hand clothes and shoes that others would give. It was these items that became our joy of experiencing "new."

Mentally and physically, I had to fight to live every single day. Literally, my oldest brother and I would physically fight daily. The reason, well there was no rhyme or reason. In my opinion, I was the outlet of his own displaced anger. I recall an evening when we were in a fight and I hit him in the head with a lamp. The scar that is left behind from this incident is that I was the one that received the rod of correction. These are the events that would leave permanent scars in my life. The times when I would keep it all inside as I did not want to become the laughingstock of the family. The times I would voice my concerns to my mother, only to hear, "You ought not to let your brother make you upset like that!" The times when the punishment seemed so displaced and unfair. It was in these moments, that I did not understand at the time, but the enemy was laying the foundations that he would need to accomplish the anticipated failure he expected for my life. Instability and being evicted from our low-income housing due to uncleanliness and rowdy crowds made me somewhat immune to hurt, pain, and disappointments in life. The instabilities of life came from not knowing one day to the next if there would be a home to live in, electricity in the home, or if the only car we had would still be there or would it have been repossessed, out of gas, or broke down. We lived in low-income housing most of my life.

Most of my memory is of the housing projects on Green Street in Tupelo, Mississippi. Most of these environments were certain to be roach-infested. I remember laying on the couch in the roach-infested apartment and a roach getting in my ear. This was very painful, shameful, and embarrassing to have to go to the local emergency room to have a roach removed out of my ear.

There were the constant questions of whether my brother would be drunk or sober on any given day. My mother received food stamps, so we always had food. The place of anguish came with wondering would we have a home or refrigeration to preserve the food. Many times, we loss months' worth of food because we were evicted and had nowhere to go or store the food we had just bought for the month! Most of my childhood years was spent in poverty and eviction.

I remember living in the projects and taking on a summer job at a small candy stand that was in the neighborhood. The owner of this establishment was a middle-aged man in his late 40's who was blind. He was glad to have this young girl working in his store, if I could keep secrets. It was here that I was first introduced to another plot that was designed to cater to the enemy's plan of failure for me. I vividly remember being told to come to the back door when I came to open the store. One morning, as I entered the back door, I was beckoned to come into a side room of the store. It was there, he [the owner] was laying on an outdoor beach chair with his genitals in the open. I was asked to--- Now, nothing was completed on my part, but I remember how violated I felt. That was the last day I worked for him, but the hardest part was the silence that came behind the whole situation. Would I tell my mother or brother? No! Why? This certainly would not have been a secret with my mother and most likely would have been a story of laughter or pain in some way. As for my brother, he would have certainly attributed this to my "fastness" as a female. I knew it would have been deemed my fault in some kind of way. There was not a father around to think about sharing this deeply, offensive event with. I tucked it away in the recesses of my heart, but I am confident that it became a wound in my soul. It was these many different chains of events that gave me justification to be angry, depressed, hurt, shamed, and reactive to life instead of proactive. Life taught me not to love or be lovable. It became my defense mechanism to live behind the wall of hurt, shame, bitterness, disappointment, and rejection.

My oldest brother was one of the major players the enemy used in his strategic plan of failure for my life. The enemy's plan consisted of creating an environment where daily I was told what the negative outcome of my life would be. My oldest brother declared that I would be "barefoot and pregnant" by the age fifteen. Having never understood true love, it was difficult for him to show me love. He expressed love by his constant verbal and physical abuse. His anger was somehow meant to portray his passionate love for myself and others. This is what he called love, but these many negative actions that he portrayed as love secured in my heart that it was not what I wanted or needed. Early on, I decided if this is what love was, I did not want it!

He validated my fears in that he never allowed me to know the security of a male figure or a big brother. At best, he helped me to embrace the demonic spirit of rejection which started in the womb. My life would be one without the input of an earthly father. For the role of the Father is one that God put in place to speak to my identity, to assure and reassure who I was created to be! Yes, that voice was absent from the start! The root of rejection was planted in the womb and the enemy would certainly use this as one of his tools in his plan for my failure and ultimate demise.

It was after the tragic house fire that my brother and I went to live with our mother in Fulton, Mississippi. It was about this same time, in 1982, my mother would have her third child and second son, again, out of wedlock. My story would get sketchy throughout these years of life. Being the product of a single parent home caused the dynamics to become quite complicated. My older brother, forced to become the father figure in our home, became the troubled teen in middle school. I remember many nights that my mom and I would ride the streets looking for him because he had not come home. The street life would afford him many occasions to be in and out of the jail cell. The paradox of my brother's story is that he was a star football player, an honor roll student and was destined to play in the National Football League. Yet, he became the statistical black male victim who would become a high school dropout and later become acquainted with multiple prison terms. Females became the target of his misplaced anger through verbal, emotional, and physical abuse; and I, unfortunately, was no exception.

We remained in Fulton, Mississippi until I was in the 4th grade, at which time we moved to Tupelo, Mississippi. In 1986, my mother would have her 4th and 3rd son by the first man that would appear to be the father figure we all secretly longed for and needed. For the first time in my life, it seemed that I would have the father that I saw many of my peers enjoy. He was a nice, laid back guy. He seemed interested in our lives and was the first glimpse of possible stability. My brother would no longer have to be the father figure in the home. I remember when he and my mother first met. Although, a single mother of four, we were not accustomed to men staying overnight at our home. I think this must have been the first and, as I recall, it was certainly the last. Of course, some time transpired, but this man spent the night once, and the next major event was the wedding. We would later learn, he was a nice man, if he were sober. We grew to love him. He was a man who cooked, cleaned, and took care of the house chores. I do not recall much about his work life, but I always remember my mother being a hard worker.

It was not long before I realized that the nights would end with me crying myself to sleep at night because of the violent bickering and fussing that would go on between my mom, stepfather, and my brother. Many of these nights often began because my stepfather would come home drunk and call my mother out of her name until she would get fed up and then she would commence with the licks. It appears all was good between my stepfather and mom until the day she found out she was pregnant. From that point on, things seemed to rapidly decline. It was the times when he was inebriated that the chaos exploded.

Mama was easy-going, stoic at best, but these years of chaos are imprinted in my brain. The usual scenario was one in which he would get drunk and the name calling would persists until my mother would become physical with him. Once she became physical, that was the end of any additional name calling or arguments for the night. This continued, almost daily, until the climax of it all. There was one day when an argument began in the kitchen. This argument escalated between he and my mother until my oldest brother became involved. With his involvement came a violent turn of events and my brother was pushed through a glass window. It was not long after this event that the marriage ended in divorce, and again, we became a single parent home, now with four children.

There was a return to the usual after the divorce, just with children who were older. The older brother stepped back in the father space, the fighting between he and I continued, the evictions and poverty mindset continued, and home was still a beacon of pain and darkness for me.

This continued until we had the second glimpse of hope for a father figure when my mom married a second time. Again, to an alcoholic, that seemed to pattern the first. They both were nice men, until they became intoxicated. And again, the cycle seemed to repeat itself only worse the second time around. One stark difference from the first stepdad would be that this man was a mechanic, and rarely took a bath. His heart was not as caring or loving as my mother's first husband. He did not seem to be as interested in us as children and our needs. He was not a housekeeper or cook and was not concerned about cleanliness as evidenced by his personal hygiene. The days of stink were, at times, overbearing. This was also the first time I was introduced to a man that ate "over-easy, runny eggs."

Money continued to be an issue. Other than mechanic jobs, I never knew this second husband to have meaningful employment that could maintain a family of six. The arguments continued and the violence grew until one day my brothers and I came home to our mother who had been hit in the head with a tire iron during a fight between her and the second husband. The doctor's report was that of a miracle considering another inch deeper and my mother could have had life altering or even an injury that resulted in death. This night ended with my older brother being cut with a knife by my stepfather, and the doctors declared that he was literally inches from losing his life had the knife cut his jugular vein.

After this episode, my brother became enraged and determined to seek revenge on the man that had injured him and our mother. It was during this time that I can remember my mother sitting quietly with her arms folded and praying to God to let her and her children make it out of this situation alive and safely. The God rescue did not come without the revenge my brother sought after. It was on a winter night that my brother approached our stepdad as he was coming in from his usual day of working on cars. We were not at home at the time of this incident to witness the events. The story told to us was one of utter trauma. My brother had worn steel toe boots as he disfigured our stepdad's face. He used a small metal air tank to physically beat him. Although, our stepdad survived this attack, he was permanently disfigured with facial swelling until his death years later. I do not recall any immediate jail time. These were days that I felt numb and mostly in denial to the dysfunctional living we endured. This was likely the time; I was old enough to begin to look for escapes from the dysfunction that had become my norm. God answered my mother's prayers. I do not recall how it all ended, but I just know one day I came home, and he was gone. As of today, my mother remains a single woman and never again remarried.

To sum it all up, life was hard and presented many challenges. I really did not know this was not normal until I was exposed to other families and able to compare my home life with that of others around me. I remember having other families around us who appeared to have a mother and father present and did not seem to ever mention fights, arguments, or utter chaos in their homes. Home seemed to be a quiet, peaceful place for those around me. Or, at least, that is what I observed. I really did not understand the impact that this dysfunctional, chaotic, poverty-stricken childhood life would have on me as I grew older, and the deliverances I would have to undergo simply to walk free of the demonic influences that would desire to control me. The enemy's plan to use my brother as a key player, the rejection that attached itself at the womb, the many days as a child forced to take on the roles of an adult were the many challenges that are constant reminders of God's plan for my life above that of the enemy.

The truths that desired to become my lifelong realities can all be traced back to these very years that I would call the life of humble beginnings. The humble beginnings of being raised in a single parent home in roach-infested housing projects. The days of standing in the long lines in the heat and cold to receive government assistance to survive. The times of eviction and no stable home to live in. The shameful life of being the poor project girl and hand-me-downs being my definition of new. The days of going without electricity. The dark days of depression. The days of wanting to know what it would be like to enjoy what other girls my age called "fun." These were my humble beginnings that were painful and shameful at the time. Of course, at the time of the events, I did not understand them to be the lessons I would need to have compassion, to understand giving from a barren place, or to be thankful and appreciative for the days I could have store bought and not second-hand donations. To this day, these life experiences afford me a heart of humility. I do not know about a life passed down through generational platters, but I certainly can identify with working for everything I now call my own!

Chapter II
Wanted But Unwanted

As a child, growing up in a single parent home, I always longed for the love of my natural father. This desire many times displayed itself as mean, sad, depressed, and living-behind-the-wall type of behaviors. These actions were clearly my own mechanisms of self-defense. The outer shell seemed extremely hard, but underneath there was a heart that simply wanted, longed for, and many times craved to be loved. An all-or-nothing kind of heart. The heart that did not know two faces and loved hard. This heart knew no boundaries and many times ended up hurt, because all it wanted was to be loved.

I grew up knowing very well how not to love myself. As a matter of fact, the only thing I liked about me was my hairy legs. The one thing that I had in my favor, was the Lord had given me brains and I could think. I was smart in school and mostly stayed to myself. I had a no-nonsense kind of personality. This personality had a face that rarely engaged in laughter. The face of a fighter, as that is what my home life consisted of in all facets. The flat face that rarely showed any emotions other than serious. While others my age were enjoying youth activities on the weekend and evening with friends, my life was in my room writing in my diary or letters to Jesus. There was not much tolerance for anything that others my age classified as "fun." This personality was birthed out of the previously discussed obligations to be an adult as a child.

Many things catered to the complexities of rejection in my life, including not having nice clothes as other children my age had. The saying "children can be cruel" was true in my life. Christmas excitement for me was getting nice hand-me-downs, and the items that came from my mother standing in the long lines to get us registered to pick-up items with Toys for Tots every year. These shameful experiences caused me to embrace being alone. I learned to not engage in the back-to-school conversations after special holidays. Instead, I would listen to others as they enjoyed talking about the many presents that Santa had brought them on Christmas including the new and expensive tennis shoes they were wearing. It was easier to focus on staying alone and not become involved, then I would not be forced to relive the depths of shame, pain, and disappointment that daily stared at me from home. My mother was not into fashion or all the "girly" things. Therefore, fashion, hair, nails, and all the things girls in their early teens desired was not a priority for me.

Although my mother was not into fashion, she made sure I knew to take a bath, but there was not much room for the things most girls my age liked to do. While girls my age were enjoying their dolls, I remember having to make sure dinner was cooked, bills were paid, and writing letters to express my feelings and remain sane during the chaos that home presented. These adult responsibilities made me long the more for a natural father's love. Somehow, I felt this was the missing link to a more stable and happier life.

In my longing to be loved by my natural father, I have one, final childhood memory of attempting to make this a reality. My biological father, a quartet singer, was known in his local community and surrounding cities. I would not see him often; maybe once every other month, and each time I would make myself known to him. I remember times I would see him and put myself in his way as to be noticed by him. Many times, this would lead to him acting as though he did not see me at all until, I would physically get in his face. One of these times happened when we were at a quartet singing event and he was on the church steps conversing with another female. I rudely approached and began a conversation with him. A very superficial conversation with the intent to be acknowledged as his daughter. There were very few words spoken before he walked away. As far as life goes and being able to say he personally provided for me, that is non-existent. These superficial conversations would sometimes lead to broken promises of coming to pick me up to spend time at his home--that never manifested. It almost seemed he would say what he felt I needed to hear to leave him alone.

This last memory and final encounter that I have of my father as a child was the one time, he picked me up and I visited his home. I had to be between the age of 10 and 12 at this time. These years and ages are lost somewhere in the subconscious mind. This opportunity, as I consider, due to its rarity and as a personal heart's desire, was shared with a sister that is a few months older than me. This was also the sister whom he loved and recognized as being his; one of his "favorites." I did not mind not being the choice daughter, so much as I simply wanted to feel as though I was wanted by my natural father.

During this time visiting him, he requested some food be warmed up for dinner. I remember him telling me to let my older sister warm up the food as "I didn't know what I was doing." As pleasant as I would have liked for this visit to have gone, it was the fire that once again fueled the already burning blaze of rejection. He had never known me, so how could he possibly know what I could or could not do at this very brief encounter? Maybe, somewhere deep inside, this was my one chance to prove myself to him. The one time he would have to know how much of a "big girl" I really was. In my mind, that would have been a perfect time to please him and perhaps he would want me. After all, we were strangers knitted by the sperm he donated to my mother, but certainly not by the ingredients needed to know the girl who was his daughter by DNA. This trip was the one opportunity he would have to show me that he loved and wanted me! Instead, it was the final encounter that solidified what was believed – that my natural father did not want me. Needless to say, a negative seed was also sown between my sister and me that day. One that my sister did not sow directly, but the root of rejection that indirectly affected what could have been a viable relationship between the two of us. Deeper than that, again, it reiterated to me that I was not good enough. I recall the food being burned during the warming process. There was much I wanted to say that would "prove" to him who I was and what I could do, but the real feelings of rejection surfaced instead, and I immediately requested to go home. Of course, he agreed, but not before he committed one last insult.

On the way home, he demanded that I spend my money to buy my sister and I something from a small country store. Why would this hurt so deeply? This is the man who was my natural father. The one who should have taught me who I was. He was the man that should have spoken to what I was to be in the earth. He should have been my provider and protector. He should have been the one making sure my needs were met, and that I knew what it looked like and felt like to be loved by a father and a man. Instead, the final demand was that I spend my money on the child that you favor?! What type of father would be so low as to ask for my money to support his other child instead of him buying us both something? What type of father has no interest in getting to know the girl he created? I was deeply hurt and offended. Well, I will leave it to your imagination as to how this scenario ended. My last words were, "Take me home and you never have to worry about me again, ever!"

The voice of hurt had spoken, and as always, I would simply pack it away in my heart and keep it moving. However, the one kind thing he did was introduce me to my oldest sister, Mildred. She was the one that spent time with me, and allowed me a relationship with her, her husband, and three boys. She wanted me in her life and seemed to love me at first sight. She made sure to pick me up to stay with her frequently and always included me in the holiday festivities growing up. Our relationship formed roots and fostered a deep bond that exists today and is the only meaningful relationship on my paternal side of the family. I do have several other brothers and sisters and our superficial relationships consist of a nice greeting and kosher chatting when we see each other in public.

I learned through rejection how not to let people "in too deep." I heard a pastor say once that people come into your life for seasons, reasons, or a lifetime. It was through rejection that all my relationships were classified as seasonal. I chose not to entertain any relationships that could possibly be in other categories. I chose not to see any relationships as reasons and not for a lifetime. Seasonal relationships helped me to better deal when people walked out of my life or when relationships caused pain. I would simply ascribe it to them only being around for a season, and when they left that season was up. After all, if your biological father does not want you, surely no one else would dare to entertain a relationship beyond that of a season, right? And again, that demonic spirit of rejection had tightened its grip of my heart and it seemed as if the wall around my heart would be continually fortified, until one day the unthinkable would happen!

I would begin to open my heart up to some things that would finally allow me the possibility of feeling wanted. There are depths to this journey, that you will continue to read, but as for now, know that I have a heavenly Father who has shown me that I was wanted before my mother and natural father ever came to know each other sexually!

Chapter III
The Expectation

Life begins with great expectations. Personally, it is hard to believe that my mother expected to give birth to a first child who grows up an alcoholic, abusive, troubled, and imprisoned. A second child who becomes a teenage mother, depressed, rejected. A third child who would be attached and unable to enjoy life outside of the confines of his mother. A fourth child who would move away and live a somewhat estranged life ---and the list could go on and on about the negative outcomes and lives that do not cater to the common societal definition of success. However, many times as parents, we underestimate the spiritual expectations that come from both good and evil forces. So, I would like to take some time and explore both aspects of the expectations that are placed on human life, even from the womb.

Naturally, I recall my mother expecting to provide us with a stable home environment.

Although birthed out of wedlock, it was not her desire for me to grow up without the love of my natural father. My mother expected for us to be grounded in our faith as she was a praying and faithful church going woman. This I witnessed with my own eyes. There were many things she could not give me, but the one thing she gave me was JESUS! Naturally, she expected me to have an education as she advocated for school and graduation. She also advocated going to college and "making something of ourselves." However, there was some expectations far deeper than what could have ever been expected in the natural, and that is where I would like to spend some time.

Spiritually, our heavenly Father has the very nature and character of love (1 John 4:7 KJV). As a matter of fact, it would not be until he had children that we could even see his heart of love displayed. Thus, we see the creation of man in Genesis 1:26 KJV, which gives us the picture of the heart of the Trinity and God's plan for mankind in the Earth. "Let us" make man in our image and in our likeness and let "them have dominion in the Earth." The Father's expectation for his children was always colonization of earth with the Kingdom of Heaven and never church.

He always desired relationship and not religion. He envisioned kingdom citizens and sonship; while the evil one set out to halt creation at servants and religious affiliations (Christianity, Muslim, Buddhism, Islam, etc.). Thus, we see the fall of mankind in the garden. Here is where Adam and Eve forfeited a kingdom. Relinquishment of this kingdom would now awaken a carnal man and all of its tendencies.

Creation would now battle on two fronts the carnal and spiritual man. It is to our carnal man, that the enemy, the Devil, Satan, our adversary, speaks his expectations. It is in our carnal man, in the depths of our soul, that we become wounded by the expectations of the evil one for us. In our weakened and unlearned state, the evil one begins to declare lies to us. According to John 8:44 (KJV), we understand the devil is the father of lies and there is no truth in him. This means ANYTHING that he speaks is a lie!

Let me just speak of some personal lies that he deceived me with. He told me at an early age that I was not loved or wanted. This spirit of rejection attached itself to me in my mother's womb through the neglect and absence of my father and gave way to other demonic attachments through this access point. I remember when Satan told me I would be better off dead, which was most of my childhood and early adult life. The entertainment of this lie gave access to the demon of depression and suicide that attached itself to me at an incredibly early age. I remember growing up, sitting in my room, writing letters to God, and crying myself to sleep at night. Longing to be wanted, loved, and accepted by anyone, at this point. I remember being forced to babysit other children while their parents lived the party life and while my childhood life was on hold. This led to the fantasy of me having a child at a young age.

I was convinced that I would have someone to love and that child would love me back. My child would need and want me! The need for love and attention led me to pursue happiness in the marijuana joint and the alcohol bottle in the confines of my own apartment at sixteen years of age. Through various areas of rejection, the enemy had convinced me I would always need to be able to depend on myself, for I was the only person that would never let "me" down. This lie would cater to my mindset of being an independent woman. I did not know at the time of embracing this lie, this would later cause strongholds in my marriage. Man, what lies the enemy made me believe! My outer expressions of the lies were wrapped in a hard, outer shell with a very fragile heart underneath. Outer expressions that consisted of very superficial relationships and walls that were seemingly unbearable to permeate. I was a loner who stayed to myself and did not bother anyone. I considered myself the "black sheep." I saw myself as the outcast and my home life was too unstable to risk becoming vulnerable in any relationship. My home life was a place of shame, pain, and hurt. I believed the more closed I was, and the harder I appeared, the less interaction I would have. The less interaction, the less risk of exposing my heart.

The unpleasant outer disposition that I displayed was a hard outer covering of the fragile inner hurt, pain, and shame. The harsh appearance of my face was used to keep anyone out that might have the potential to hurt me. After all, I had learned that people were a source of hurt and the less interaction I had with people, the less potential for more hurt. The enemy EXPECTED for me to fail, but little did I know, my heavenly father had already DESTINED for me to succeed. Him being eternal, stepped outside of time and aligned some strategic appointments in time that would all lead to some particularly important dates.

Chapter IV
Dates With Destiny

What is seen with the naked eye is usually deeper than one could ever perceive without the spirit of God to give insight! This profound statement was nowhere to be comprehended at the tender age of fifteen, when I seemed to realize life began to unfold into the purpose of God for me. Yes, as a teenage mother, is where it all began to make sense! It, being the plan of God for my life. It was the parenting life I had fantasized about that now was a reality! The fantasy that I would have a child that would need and want me! I now had a real human being, other than myself that totally depended upon me to be and do everything. Yes, he was real and not just a figment of my imagination! That meant I had to make some life decisions, and at the time, I had no clue of what that would look like.

Destiny was my secret admirer. I was fifteen when I realized I had a secret admirer since I was born. Someone who had always admired me and loved me! He had chased me all these years and finally I was willing to really get to know him. The courtship was made official when Romans 10:9 became my revelation truth. He began to offer me many surprises and each of them changed my life permanently in many ways. Now, let me be clear, I am writing in retrospect, as at the time, I did not realize these were, in fact, dates with destiny!

So, let us begin this amazing story of manifold love, hopefully, not repeating much of what has already been stated. In all the previous chapters, I attempted to open my heart up to show you all the ways I was exposed to things that threatened failure in life. Those openings justified me looking for temporary ways to feel loved and wanted. One of those ways was the loss of my virginity around the age of nine. The specifics of such a life-changing event escape my mind, but I remember the guy (older than I) and I remember the wooden house located in the hills of the country.

Remember, my mother worked a lot, and my brother was an alcoholic, so it was not hard for someone to catch me in a vulnerable state and pay me some attention. Any attention, at that age, seemed better than the negativity I was getting at home. And there in the quietness of the countryside, my innocence was given to the first guy who would introduce me to sexual intercourse. While the act of intercourse was brief in time, it was certainly permanent in what was spiritually introduced to a nine-year-old baby girl who was already struggling to define real love.

A young girl who was smart, athletic, and loved school, but was rejected, verbally and physically abused, and carrying excessive adult responsibilities; looking for attention and love was my way of escape from the chaos at home. At the time I did not realize this is what was happening, however, as I grew and understood more, I soon realized my search was for true love, but I sought it in the wrong places. Ironically, I do not remember much regarding my school years. I am unsure of why there is no recollection of much of my school years, although I am confident it was buried in my subconscious mind as to forget the pain that was associated with those years of my life. If I had to sum up those years of childhood and school age years, I would use descriptive words such as sad, painful, hurtful, shameful, depressing, and lost to say the least.

These were years that I wondered, "Why was I even allowed to be born? Why would I be dealt such a harsh hand in life?"

I had no revelation of the destiny that awaited me. I had no revelation that life was simply preparing me to be who God had created me to be in the earth. As a matter of fact, these thoughts in the moment, never crossed my mind. I now understand that many of our outward actions and reactions stem from the subconscious mind. You know, those times when we have angry outburst that do not fit the situation at hand? Or the times we respond inappropriately or in displaced anger and it does not fit the current situation? I have two significant memories that stand out during my school years. My 4th grade teacher at Fulton Elementary School named Ms. Stubblefield. Why she is embedded in my memory, I do not know, but she is. Honestly, I only remember her calm and caring personality. I can still see the depth of her heart that seemed to portray her care and love for her students as she looked me in my eyes. I remember her sweet smile and her simple touch. Perhaps, she represented a sense of peace away from the storm for me. Her family was known in the town of Fulton, MS, but I only know of her love and care for her students. School was an escape from the verbal and physical abuse at home. Her classroom seemed to be a place of peace and calm away from the chaos. I looked forward to going to her classroom and experiencing her serenity.

The next introduction that would have an impact was my 6th grade school counselor at Carver Elementary School, Dr. Debra Calvert. This encounter taught me the short time it takes to make a lifelong impact. She was one of few people that saw my heart and affirmed the hidden heart that she saw. She was one of the people who let me know that I had meaning and value. She was also one of the people who said I would be something great when I grew up. I am not sure how she picked me out, other than divine unction. She stopped me one day in the hall and told me she needed some office help. She allowed me to assist her in her office doing minor clerical work and filing paperwork.

On one occasion after school, she took me to her home, allowed me to meet her husband and two boys and took me to her evening church service. It may not seem like much, but this simple, yet profound gesture of concern impacted my life forever. It was her simple gesture to include me, unplanned, in her life that made me feel loved, wanted, and needed. I felt special! After all, I lived in the projects, but it was a big ordeal to be the counselor's office assistant. Not just any counselor, but Dr. Calvert. These acts of care and concern would be a permanent reminder of a lady who saw my heart and declared that I would grow up to be something in life. I would later learn she was well-loved and respected in her workplace and community. Her husband was and still is a well-known insurance agent. Dr. Calvert showed me another glimpse of true love. To be honest, school was the only time I got an inkling of what a girl my age should be doing. After the school days ended, it was back to the verbally and physically abusive brother that was dealing with his own issues, including that of assuming adult roles as a child. After school was the responsibility of cooking dinner, figuring out the bills, and helping younger siblings. Many times, I was left raising other children that my mother had taken in while their parents lived and enjoyed the club life, and I was trying to keep a clean and livable environment in hopes we would not be evicted.

After Carver School, we moved to Verona, MS and I attended Verona Middle School my

7th and 8th grade school year. It was during this time my mother was married to her second husband. I played for the Jr. High and High School basketball team during my 8th grade school year. I came from a family of athletes and was blessed to play multiple sports. I played softball during the summers with community summer leagues. I specifically remember playing a summer of softball and becoming the youngest player of the girls that were high school age and older. This incident is included simply because I believe it was the foreshadow of a key person in my life's story named Joseph Hawkins, who pastors a church in Starkville, MS. The memories of this event were strategically aligned to give me a negative view of any mentions of Starkville, MS. I remember a visit to Starkville, MS to visit the summer softball coach. I recall this incident because this would be the first time, I knew what it was to be intoxicated. Intoxication was the result of hanging with other players who were older than me and able to buy alcohol. I seem to have been the only one that was intoxicated on this trip and the feeling was very unpleasant to say the least.

The Jr. High basketball years were intermittently happy as I finally found a place where I felt I belonged. During these years, I met the guy who would become my first love, at the approximate age of thirteen and later my oldest child's father at age fifteen. He was four years older than I was when our relationship began. He and his family were from the Delta area and had recently relocated to Verona, MS. We were neighbors. We began spending evenings together and it did not take long before we were involved sexually. By this time, he was a glimpse of someone who would appear to want and love me. As I focused on my fantasy to have a child that I could love and that would love me back, we began to have sexual encounters several times a day. After being forced to care for other children my mother would take in, I believed I could raise a child of my own. I was not the most fertile chick as getting pregnant took some time! During this relationship, there was no real discussion of life plans or us wanting children. He seemed to be love and attention, as well as an escape from my older brother.

At this time, I was in the 7th or 8th grade at Verona Jr. High, and for the first time in my life, I would meet someone I would call a friend---a female friend that I could share my life with. I would find myself spending the evenings after school at her house. I would be able to play sports with someone who I could finally associate with and not have to hide my true life from. She would be the only person, other than a boyfriend, that I would share a glimpse of my heart with. Unfortunately, it was with this same female friend that I experienced a hurt that built a wall and closed my heart off to friendship.

It was the usual evening routine that my boyfriend, myself, and my new best friend would spend together. As all boyfriend/girlfriend relationships have times of misunderstanding and temporary breakups, this one was not exempt. During one of the breakups, my best friend and boyfriend began dating. This did not last long and before you knew it, he and I were back together; however, it did not end without a physical fight and permanent separation of the only female friendship I had known in my life. This, again, left a permanent wound in my soul. Even through all the drama, I was not yet in a place where I knew who I was in Christ. I was still willing to settle for the feeling of being wanted or told "I love you!" Thus, we resumed our sexual life, and I resumed my pursuit to get pregnant. Later, his family would be moving back to their home in the Delta and we would move to Pontotoc, MS for my start of the 9th grade. My boyfriend did not want to move back to the Delta and needed somewhere to stay, so he ended up moving in with us. Now this allowance speaks to a mother who was an enabler. She was stoic, but tended to be easy going at times that may have needed more firmness. This was not different from the many other live-ins we had during our childhood. My mother was known for always having someone else's children living with her. There really did not have to be a legitimate reason, simply a person that said they needed a place to stay…as was the reason when my boyfriend moved in with us. Of course, this presented the perfect alignment to become pregnant, as we were in a relationship and he became close to my oldest brother. His relationship with my oldest brother made the move-in easier. They both were accustomed to the street hustle. The one whom I had come to love spent his days enjoying the streets while I was six months pregnant scrubbing the floors of a McDonald's restaurant for a living. It was after the 9th grade school year I chose to drop out of school and in my sixth month of pregnancy my boyfriend and I called it quits for good.

It is here the word collision comes into play. According to a google search, collision is defined as an instance of one moving object or person striking violently against another. This is exactly what was happening with my life and destiny. The two were beginning to have head-on collisions. Did I know it at the time? Of course not! I was a "church baby." Raised in the Baptist faith, my mother was faithful to church all our lives. Remember, she was the one who really gave me Jesus! This was key to some upcoming encounters that would later play out to be divine dates with destiny.

My church memberships, that I recall, began during my mother's first marriage. I attended a church called St. Matthew Missionary Baptist Church in Fulton, MS. It was here I was introduced to Pastor Marquette and First Lady Linda Rogers. My mother was known to love, follow, and show great care and concern for her leaders. Many times, people would be inclined to help my mother as she was the single mother raising four children. As the only girl, I remember Lady Linda Rogers making it her business to spend time with me. I remember one weekend when she took me to her home in Guntown, MS. It was something about this lady, that in my immature mind, I would not be able to articulate until years later. Years later would introduce me to the

Apostolic anointing that was on her life, but I would not understand until we would reconnect again in my married, adult life.

Later, I was a member of White Hill Baptist Church, a little small church located in the vicinity of the projects in Tupelo, MS. My mother was always one of the "Amen" women in the church and I sang in the church choir. As a member of this Baptist church, we were not one of the in-crowd people, but were casually received and superficially known. It was in the middle of 1994 (around April or May) that our church went on a church trip to Wisconsin. The trip had no significant events, other than upon our return, the news was delivered that the church organist, Daryl, was in the hospital. It was said that he was extremely sick and had AIDS. Again, the start of a collision.

This devastating news led me to being a caretaker for Daryl, a guy who I barely knew, and who would later become my God-brother. This opportunity came by simply visiting this person I knew as my church organist in the hospital after that church trip. I was told the severity of the situation, but did not know the magnitude of where this one visit would lead. When another church member and I arrived at the hospital to visit him, he was alone. Of course, my caring heart could not leave him there sick and alone. This hidden side of my heart, which no one saw often, certainly could not and would not allow that. The fact that I was now six months pregnant was not an issue for him, so, I stayed. I stayed the duration of his two-to-three-week hospital admission, and he asked the regretted question, "Will you go home with me?" My first response was, "Your mother would not allow this." However, as our relationship grew, I was given the opportunity to see his family dynamics.

Daryl was adopted at the age of eighteen by a nurse's assistant who was well-known and respected in the hospital setting as "Nurse Williams." She was the only nurse's aide allowed by the hospital to dress in her crisp, starched, white uniform on every shift she worked. She was married to a husband who suffered from Bipolar Disorder and many other health issues. She also cared for her mentally ill mother-in-law, niece, and sickly sister-in-law who lived across the street from her. She had no children of her own, but was more than glad to include anyone else Daryl loved. She would many times thank me for being with him in the hospital and she, too, began to make plans for me to come home with them after he was discharged. Soon, it was noticeably clear, and the decision was made. I went home with Daryl when he discharged, and our lives intertwined so much so that his mother became my mother! Nurse Williams became my "Mama Williams." I felt needed and wanted. It was the first time I identified with the heart of a caretaker and realized; I was good at doing the job. This was certainly a foreshadow of what was to come! The significance of all this… went something like this….

Over the eight months I was privileged to care for him while he was terminally ill, I watched the toll that AIDS took on Daryl's body and his vision. He was blind and, on most days, very weak. There were days when he would get out of bed and we would go to the piano. He would play and we would sing until he was too weak to sit up anymore. He became the big brother I longed for but never really had. He would challenge me to find words daily and tell him what they meant. He knew I had something in the brain that needed to be stimulated. He would speak daily into my life. One way he showed me he loved and cared for me, was his care, concern, and attention to how I presented myself. Although, physically blind, he wanted to make sure I got up every day and put on something nice to wear. To achieve this, he picked clothes from his closet for me to wear and then he would tell me how beautiful I was in them. But how did he know how beautiful I was or how nice I looked in his outfits, considering he was blind? Never, in the moment, did I realize what God was doing in my life. He was building my confidence and my self-esteem through a male voice I had never had in my life. He was reaching to the hard, walled, places in my heart and preparing them to receive the love that was on its way from many directions. Daryl was the reason my oldest child would have three names instead of the usual two. He longed for a child named "DeBrico" and we knew, in his dying state, that would never be his reality.

Thus, my child is named DeBrico Shanques Terrell. It was my dying angel's dream fulfilled. My child was born October 10, 1994. After having my baby, I went back to my mom's house for a short time. During this time, Daryl and I kept in touch by phone and as soon as the healing was completed, I was able to resume care for him. This care did not last much longer as he would soon pass in March of 1995. Childbirth was long and hard. After receiving an epidural that slowed my labor and having a hard labor, I remember being nauseated at the time of push. With every gag, there would be a vaginal cut. This ended with an 8 lb., 9-ounce baby boy, thirty-five plus sutures, and massive breast engorgement upon discharge. I would lay flat my back for the whole allotted six weeks with little activity, other than what was necessary.

    I remember the night after having my baby, I was on the phone and the nurse walked in. She questioned who I was on the phone with. You guessed it; it was Daryl. In the wee hours of the morning, I was on the phone with Daryl, the first person that showed me the true love of a brother. Although he had physical limitations, he was not bound in his heart. It was his heart of detail, care, and concern; his daily attention to making sure that I did something productive with my brain. It was how he cared about how I was feeling as a teenage mother and made himself open to have heart-to-heart conversations. He was the male voice, the big brother voice that wanted to protect me even with his physical limitations. He was making sure I was doing well after giving birth. He was my outlet. He understood me! He was the first male that gave me permission to be me and he genuinely loved the raw me! He accepted me for me! I did not have to fake it; I was free to be me!

We developed a bond that came through shedding of tears and hard conversations. Of course, he became attached, as I became his primary caregiver. We slept in the same bed, him at the head and me at the foot. Never one time was I concerned about being violated. He loved me enough to share his heart with me. I was the only one he verbally admitted his AIDS diagnosis to. He simply cared. He wanted the best for me within the realm of what he could give. He gave me his time, his heart, his intelligence. He taught me lessons about the importance of being presentable in public. Many times, he spoke to my confidence and where I would be in life. He did not want anything from me, we were attached at the heart, and this collision yet lives with me today.

After becoming pregnant, breaking up with my baby's father at six months of pregnancy, and becoming a primary caretaker to my god-brother who was terminally ill, eventually, I lived the fantasy as my reality became this fifteen-year-old baby raising my own baby. Although I was mature for my age at that time, I was still yet, very immature, regarding knowing how to raise a baby and maneuver life at this age.

I had made the decision not to go back to school the upcoming year and had just come through the loss of my friend and divine brother. With a child to care for, I began to give thought to my plans for the future. These plans involved my first apartment at the age of sixteen and a job at local grocery store as a cashier – which I will expound on later. My mother was very instrumental in assisting with childcare during this time. To make ends meet, I had worked a part-time job at Sonic and endured working a full-time job and scrubbing the floors at McDonalds at six months of pregnancy, while my child's father was hanging out with the boys and enjoying the street life.

My child's father had moved back to the Delta and was a fleeting thought by this time. By now, I had the autonomy and I had learned to hide the pain behind introversion, isolation, choice sex, drinking, getting high off marijuana, surface relationships, meanness, and the thick wall around my heart.

I recall the one time my child and I were asked to visit his father at his home in the Delta. During this visit as bad as this encounter seemed, this is when my child's father, whom I thought I loved with everything, attempted to hit me with his six-month-old son in my lap. Now, I had experienced many heartaches and let downs in both relationships and life, but the physical abuse would be more than I could handle. It was in that instant, with my infant son in my lap, that I realized what I perceived as love was not that at all. Everything I once called love, felt was love, and referenced as love - left in that moment. I have always felt Daddy God did this in an instant. He knew this was one piece of baggage I would not need to take into the future with me.

Sadly, it seemed as though the generational cycle of children out of wedlock and single parenting would be the course for me as well. However, I would adhere to one of the lessons I learned from my mother with my son. I can honestly say, my mother never painted a negative image of my biological father. She never talked to me about how bad of a person he was or his downfalls. My perception of him came from my personal encounters with him. The only thing she would ever say to me about my father is that he was not a gossiper. She would tell me how he was not a man that would snurl his nose or look down on people thought to be of lesser status. He was a clean-cut, thin, tall nice-looking man. Anything negative I knew of him, would not come from my mother. I took this same stance for my son. I was not the mother who would pursue child support. In my opinion, he did not work when I was with him, what would change now? I was not ever going to keep him from his son. He would always have the choice to establish his own relationship. I would not spend time speaking negative to my son about his father. My mother did not teach me how to do this and that is one lesson I am grateful not to have learned.

    By now, I have my own apartment, raising my son and doing my own thing apart from God, and another collision with destiny happens. I was always a thinker in the quiet times. I was one who would evaluate life and come up with a plan for the future. One of these times of deep thought, I remember looking at my child and questioning, "How can I tell him to finish school if I don't?" In that moment, I had no idea where this thought-provoking question would originate, but in hindsight, destiny was having an unsolicited conversation with me! Wow, that simple realization, began some of my next, very strategic, God-ordained collisions with destiny. The first step was going and enrolling in the local high school, which was Tupelo High School since I no longer lived in Pontotoc, MS. That is literally ALL I did, and the rest was divinely ordered.

After enrollment, I was "found" by the high school counselor Karen King-Givhan. God had a way of having the counselors find me! She told me how my transcript grabbed her attention. She noticed a year with all A's and B's, then no grades at all, and now this transcript was before her. Wow! How do you shuffle through hundreds of transcripts and this one gets your attention? Her exact words to me were, "If you do everything I tell you to do, you will graduate with your class."

The decision to go back to school and work a part-time job called for some temporary adjustments to fulfill this goal. I made the decision to move back in with Mama Williams while finishing up high school. This seemed to be the win-win solution at the time. Mama Williams was lonely and wanted someone in the home with her. She had become accustomed to having me there when Daryl was living. It was also a convenience for her, as Mama Williams did not drive. Having me around fulfilled her need of transportation and being able to handle things that required transportation. My mother was instrumental in keeping my son while I finished school and continued to help Mama Williams. Our families were eventually intertwined in every way. But before graduation would come God was aligning some other divine connections.

Now, one must understand that I had no say in my class schedules or anything when I enrolled back into school. I was literally given a schedule by Ms. King and whatever classes were listed on the schedule, that is where I showed up. It was during these school days and my participation in Air Force ROTC that I would be introduced to a man lovingly called, at the time, Sergeant Hawkins. Little did I know, at the time, this man was strategically positioned by the Father to have an impact on my life. Sergeant Hawkins was, and still is, the Pastor of Peter's Rock Family Worship Center in Starkville, MS. A pastor who has an enormous heart for youth, especially troubled youth. Somehow, he made his way into my heart. He was the first natural man that exemplified what a father's love should be.

For me, he became the male voice of the heavenly Father's affirmation and the voice of a male friend. He was the first man that listened to my heart and clearly knew the outer shell was in no way representative of the true person the Father had destined me to be. He was the first man that spoke to the spirit man of Ty. He was the first one that awakened purpose in me. He was the one that corrected the lies the evil one had been telling me all my life. He would correct things like "all men are not dogs." He was the one who made me realize that love is blind, and it is important that I understand that. He was the one that made me realize that hurt is the thing that will cause your love to become perverted and if I did not change my view of love, I would be found in the perversion of lesbianism. All because, I viewed men as dogs. This, of course, was based on my own, personal experiences. He plowed and continued to prepare my heart for the love takeover that was on the way!

I could sense the harsh walls being softened at every daily conversation with Sergeant Hawkins. These conversations would keep me levelheaded and stable. The Lord had sent Ms. King and Sergeant Hawkins to be the instruments that would help me to the graduation stage.

Of all places, I found myself a part-time cashier in a local grocery store while working to finish school. It was there at a very disoriented time in my life, a time when I was literally surviving, another date was happening. After all, who was I? Who was I to know what I liked, wanted, or needed? I knew I had to work and provide for my son and this is what I found myself trying to do (or so I thought). So, I am working a shift and I am introduced to this woman named Teresa. Remember, I am very introverted and would not dare make any attempts to show the real me. But somehow, Teresa was able to continue to water the seeds that had been planted. She would talk to me about life and eventually invited me to her church. What a small thing this would seem. It took two significant things happening, that really got my attention and, I ended up at her church.

One day we were in the store and the storm clouds begin to form. In that moment, the clouds appeared to be the darkest, blackest, most vicious clouds I had ever witnessed. In that instant, I felt something tugging at my heart. There was an eerie feeling that focused my attention on an eternal, soul searching question. "What if this is the end of time, am I ready?"

My fearful response was "No!" I do not recall the time frame between the events, but the next tug was driving home on the bypass after completing a work shift and the hood of my car flew up and blocked my view. I was not harmed, but I heard something say, "Strike three and you are out!" This saying caused a holy fear to rise in me and I knew I did not have long to make Jesus Lord!

Being raised in church, I had received water baptism at an early age. The following week of the last scare, I made my way to the little, old, two-story white church called Victory Temple Holiness Church (VT) in Tupelo, MS under the leadership of Pastor Willie G. and Lady Dorothy Thornton. It was there this 16-year-old, lost, teenage mother received Jesus and the baptism of the Holy Ghost. Oh! What a change he (Jesus) made in my life. I returned home after this service and could hardly wait to let Sergeant Hawkins know what had taken place over this weekend. The Lord allowed me to connect to this ministry as he knew some things that were transitioning that I did not yet know.

Sergeant Hawkins would soon announce that he would be leaving the school before my class was to graduate, but he assured me he would be in attendance of our graduation ceremony. This was a bitter-sweet time in my life, but it was the first time that leaving did not seem like a seasonal release. This was the first time a man that had my heart left and I did not feel dropped. He tried to prepare me for his leaving. He explained to me that God was calling him in another direction. He assured me that he would not miss the important event of my graduation. This leaving felt different from any other leaving I had experienced before now. This became my first view of how real love behaves. God did not leave me without what I needed in the time.

It was at VT, the Father taught me how to encourage myself. It was in this ministry I learned to encourage myself. Fresh out of the disorientations of life, I did not need a deep, profound, oratorical message. I simply needed to know that Jesus loves me, and he wants the best for my life. I needed to be healed. I needed to be loved. I needed to be shown that Jesus wanted me. This was the perfect place. For at Victory Temple, the Thornton's had a way of making the least of the least feel loved and wanted by Jesus. Pastor Thornton has a ministry of encouragement. He was a fisherman by nature and God used him to catch me! He did not try to clean me up, he simply loved me until I learned to do as David did in 1 Samuel 30:6 (KJV), encourage myself in the Lord. I did not anticipate that working in a local grocery store would be the date that would introduce me to my heavenly Father (the only Father I know), his son Jesus, and the Holy Spirit. How could I have arranged all the events that had to occur for me to be in this little white church and receive the gift of eternal life? I did not know that from my time with Daryl until now he was softening my heart to be able to simply hear and open my heart to the call of love! I was able to serve at this ministry for about two years before the next date would happen. This one consisted of meeting the love of my life, Mr. Harold Walton, and the rest is yet to be told for this divine connection would take me further--ready or not!

Chapter V
Ready or Not

Ready or not, here I come. I remember playing hide and seek as a child. And there would be a person tasked with finding the other children. We would be allotted a short time to hide before the countdown would begin and the seeker would declare, "Ready or not here I come!"

This encounter begins with a visitation to a church for an evening musical in November 1996. I attended this service in its entirety with my two-year-old child. At the end of the service, I returned to my vehicle that would not start. With no mechanical skills, I began to seek out someone who could help me. I was instructed to go inside the church and ask for a man named "Skip." I was directed to a tall, clean-cut, brown skinned guy. I approached him with this immediate question, "Do you have some jumping cables?" His response, "Hi, how are you?" Again, the question was asked, "Sir, do you have some jumping cables?" At the time, that was my only focus. I had no room for any additional attention, other than the question at hand. I was rude, to say the least. I continued to explain to him that my car would not start. He, being who he was and is, walked out to my car and did what God-anointed mechanics do. He gave me a jump and he asked me to allow my car to sit idle to build up the battery for about fifteen minutes or so. During this time, he asked me if I would like to go get something to eat. Immediately, in my skepticism toward males and fragile heart, I felt like this guy thought I was slow and not onto his game. Any who, not sure why my answer was yes, but we ended up dropping my child off with my Mom and heading to the Waffle House. I recall ordering an orange juice and the restaurant was out of straws. This stranger I just met kindly walked across the street to a store and bought a pack of straws. After all that, I ended up not drinking the orange juice. He followed me home and we sat out in the car and talked for several hours.

This would be my first spiritual encounter with a demon called Lust! As we sat in the car talking, this demon began to manifest. The demonic manifestation took on the form of a different face, a different voice, and immediately

I recognized this was a different person than the one who was in front of me. Having no knowledge of my call to spiritual warfare as a babe in Christ, I remember saying calmly but with confidence, "That's demonic and you need to deal with that!" Immediately, the demonic manifestation ceased, and things returned to normal. The conversation ended with a string of apologies for the manifestation and I went in the house for the night and he left. That demonic encounter would prove to be vital in the days ahead. This spirit was not violent, and it was submissive to the voice of God. There were no more sexual advances or attempts until one last time when this demon manifested, and I begin to flirt with this demon instead of standing in my place of authority. That was the first time a sexual encounter would occur outside of marriage since my salvation.

As the days progressed, we talked every day. We discussed his childhood upbringing. We identified how lust was a generational curse that went back generations in his family. He was told at the age of six, "if you want a woman, you have to take her." It was in the days ahead we both began to understand our meeting was for more than what it appeared on the surface. Did we know the depths of what this would entail? No! Yet, we both knew there was a greater purpose to our connection. Yes! It had to be strategic and divine! These everyday conversations led to more time together and overnight stays at Mama Williams. Remember, Mama Williams was known for adopting people and pulling them close.

In many ways, I felt him being there also fulfilled her void of Daryl. However, being newly saved and baptized with the Holy Ghost, this situation would pose a great conflict between my soul and spirit. The conflict would be the provisions made for the flesh and abstaining from fornication. My personality is one of "all or none" and my surrender to a saved life was nothing less. In my heart, I was ready to live totally for Christ. With this persuasion, discussions of marriage were in order as I certainly did not want to die and go to hell and he had begun to take part in important events in my life such as my senior portraits. Yep, we took them together.

It was April 1997, one month before graduating high school, destiny declared ready or not here I come with my first child about to turn three years old and an introduction to the thirty-four-year-old man who would become my husband at the age of 18. Was this teenage mother with baggage ready to be married? No! Did I know what it meant to be a wife? No! Did I marry to be divorced? No! Did I understand this was a lifelong commitment till "death do my part?" Yes! Did I know I was about to be made the Warrior I was born to be? Certainly not! Did, I fully understand the vow at such young age? No!

Before the start of the marriage, I forfeited many things as I simply wanted to please God. I forfeited most girl's dreams of a long-anticipated, elegant wedding. I forfeited knowing what it means to be courted and surprised with dates. I forfeited romance and really experiencing what that is. I forfeited the long-term courtship of getting to know him as a friend, a travel partner, and experiencing the romantic engagement. I forfeited the time-of-my-life honeymoon. Honestly, I do not know what any of these events feel like as I forfeited them all because I did not want to be living with a man I was not married to and having intermittent, pre-marital sexual encounters. This went totally against the philosophy of our belief system. He had announced his call to the ministry in 1996 and with pleasing God at the forefront of our hearts, we were married on Monday, April 14, 1997 before a yearly revival service at his church Temple of Compassion and Deliverance (TCD). We attended church service and went back to Mama Williams' house for the night. We decided to have a reception two weeks later at my church, VT. I wore a wedding dress, and the reception was small and intimate. My honeymoon consisted of going home and sleeping in peace with the man who was now my husband and not just an intermittent sexual partner.

The first transition of marriage was our decision to attend his church Temple of Compassion and Deliverance Church under the leadership of Bishop Clarence and Elder Mary Parks. My husband and I announced our call to the ministry under this leadership. It was under this leadership that the Lord showed his compassion for me and would teach me church administration and reveal the areas of needed deliverance. Oh, I thank him for his mercy and grace during these fragile years of my life.

We then moved into a small two-bedroom house in Tupelo, MS with him, myself, my son, and quickly I learned that I was pregnant with my second child and our first child together. He worked in a factory as a lineman and his job was very strenuous. He was adamant that he did not want me to work in the beginning of our marriage. This was hard for me having learned to be a very independent woman for most of my life. And less than a month into the marriage, the first argument happened.

It was summertime and he worked in the furnace area of the factory. The temps could rage over 100 degrees Fahrenheit for extended amounts of time during the day. The area was called the "knock-out room." He would frequently come home exhausted at the end of the day. I was a housewife and held the full responsibilities of the house. I would prioritize having his dinner ready when he got home. This day, pregnant and all, I stood over the stove to prepare him a good southern meal. The meal consisted of pig feet, pinto beans, corn bread, and the workings that accompany a good southern meal. I was proud of myself for persevering and cooking a meal full of love-one he would certainly enjoy! Wrong! His first words were, "Don't you know it's too hot for this type of meal?" From a heart of anger and in full attack mode, my response was, "From here on out, you can and will cook your own meals." And for a very extended amount of time, the kitchen and fixing meals was no longer my priority.

The next argument happened within the next month. This argument occurred because he went to visit his family in Amory, MS. His version of the story is this. He says he lost track of time while visiting and talking with his brothers and he arrived home after 12 midnight. I was waiting for him on the couch when he walked through the door. There was no discussion when he entered the house. I simply met him with a physical punch to the groin. His reflective response was a hit back to the face. I remained calm and went to the kitchen and began to boil some water on high. I could hear him on the phone, in the other room, calling some of my family members telling them to come get me (the fool) as I had lost my mind! I turned the boiling water off and told him not to worry about me doing anything to him right now. As I would wait until the opportunity presented itself to get revenge for the physical interchange that had occurred. Years later, he shared with me how he would sleep on high alert as he never knew when or if I was going to harm him. Let me interject here, we were both saved and Holy Ghost-filled believers! Yes, saved, but certainly not delivered!! What a sad state to be in.

Then there was the argument that happened because I asked him for money to buy groceries. He gave me $50.00. This would not have been an issue had our upbringing not been different. He was accustomed to shopping by the week. I only knew how to shop by the month. All my life we received government assistance.

When we got our food stamps for the month, mom and I would grocery shop for the month. So, when I was given $50.00 to shop for the month, I was royally offended. Not only was I offended, but I immediately begin to question his ability to provide one of my basic needs - food. I had married a man that would not be able to feed me, not to mention the two children we had at the time. It was after this episode; I begin to search out things I could do to bring income in the home. It was my desire to become an accountant for most of my high school years. However, I had an awful high school accounting teacher that made me totally lose interest. So, instead, I chose to go to a short class to become a certified nurse's assistant (CNA) and took a job working at a local nursing home. An earlier foreshadowing of life had begun to come to the horizon. I worked as a CNA and absolutely loved my job. I loved giving baths and making the patients feel like they were loved and respected.

The first five years of my marriage were treacherous, hard, and literally a crucifixion of my flesh. It was a total culture shock and continuous questioning of such a permanent decision. These were the years, unbeknown to me, the Father was unveiling the call of the warrior, deliverance, and intercession on my life. These were the years; the Lord was revealing to me what true forgiveness looked like. These years were bitter, victimizing, and certainly not what I viewed as marriage. These were the years I encountered demonic forces who presented themselves as different faces but the same human body.

The frequent manifestations of the demonic spirit of lust became a frequent tension in our marriage. The first major incident I recall happened during a very unfortunate time in my life. Our daughter was admitted to the hospital. While in the hospital with my daughter, my natural father had been killed in a work accident. At the time, my husband had changed jobs from the first factory and now worked at another local factory making more money with better benefits. He worked with my aunt on this job. He learned of the news when my aunt was called to the office for a family emergency. When he learned that her brother, who was my Dad, had been killed in a farm accident, he immediately left to come inform me at the hospital. When he arrived, I went downstairs to the Emergency Department where I met with other dramatic, grieving family members. It had been hours, by this time, and my Dad had already been taken to Jackson, MS for an autopsy.

When I returned to my daughter's room, there was a female church member visiting. I walked in the room and this person was coming out of the bathroom along with my husband. It was obvious, they had been in the bathroom together with the door closed. Missing many of the cues, during all that was happening, it was not until a few weeks later all the happenings of this day would be exposed. As newlyweds, we were called into our first meeting with our church leaders and the other female member was present. It was said, she was "dropping off diapers to my baby when the encounter occurred." This would be my first encounter with true forgiveness. To this day, unless you were involved, you would not know that the same female that attended service and worked closely beside me in the ministry was involved sexually with my husband. There would be no more up close and personal interactions, but there was nothing in my heart.

Personally, I once had a thought come to my heart, "What if marriage is to make you whole and not comfortable?" What a question so soon after a lifelong vow! A girl's heart should still be basking in the highlights of the honeymoon.

Then next challenge, which was still exceedingly early in our marriage was that my husband was hurt on his job. The job he had been at just shy of two years. Also, during this time, I was pregnant with our second and last child together and was having issues with falling. We had now moved to our second home in Verona, MS which was a trailer. I had just taken on a job working as a CNA in home health. I was on the job one day and fell going back to my car from a patient's home. Upon reporting the incident, I was not allowed to work in the field any longer and had not been on the job long enough to receive any benefits during my leave. This led to both of us being out of work without any benefits. Here we are, married for about two years, and neither of us have a job. We have one child in the home and one on the way. We transitioned into another apartment during this time and it was in this place, the Lord revealed himself to me as Jehovah Jireh. My husband was injured on his job in 1999 and I gave birth to our last son on February 18, 2000. We now had a family of two adults and three children in the home and a total of eight with our blended family. There were times when the other children would be in the home as well. Oh, what an overwhelming chain of events that had occurred in such a short time. Newlyweds, ongoing demonic issues of lust, babies ages seven, three, and a newborn; no working adults in the home and the responsibilities of adulthood before us---something had to break!

These were the years the Lord told me I could either "get up for 5 A.M. prayer and live" or "I could lay in bed and die!" Out of obedience to God, I would get up for 5:00 A.M. prayer and go in the bathroom and cry out to God. I would cry out to him to make a way for us. I believed him that we would not be without anything we needed. It was there in prayer; I begin to see God make supernatural provision for us. I recall a time when we needed food for dinner. I looked in the freezer and there was a half package of hamburger meat. I looked in the cabinet and there was one can of food. I remember standing over the stove and asking God to feed my family of five with what was in my hand. All I remember was that these were some of the best meals and I do not recall us ever being hungry. I remember a time we were out of tissue and had no money. Tissue cost less than $1.00, but that was more than we had. I remember being on my menstrual cycle and needing hygiene products. I had no hygiene products or tissue. But the one thing I had, was faith in God that he would provide. The one holiday I remember was a Christmas that we had prepared all our children. We had told them that we would not have gifts that year, but we would eat, and God would grant us his peace and joy during that year. It was Christmas Eve and Elder Mary Parks asked, "Do your kids have Christmas?" I am not sure a response was given before a credit card was given and we shopped for all our children. I remember that being one of the best holidays and oh the joy in the eyes of children who were prepared for nothing, but received something on Christmas morning.

As things were developing spiritually, other things were transpiring in the natural. God's mighty hand had sustained us through the years of 1999- 2002. After many medical visits, worker's comps disappointments, and seemingly not being able to make it another day - the settlement for his back injury happened and we were able to buy our first home. The need for money had led me to becoming a Licensed Practical Nurse (LPN). I absolutely loved caring for others. Although, growing-up, I wanted to be an accountant, the Lord had always had other plans. Things seemed to be settling and there seemed to be relief in sight. At least he was now getting disability and I was on a steady job. While things were unfolding in the natural, there were many things transpiring in the spirit that were yet years from being revealed. The Lord's plans had continued to order my steps and I found myself completing schooling and receiving my Associate degree in Nursing in 2005. I took a job as a registered nurse on a medical-surgical floor at the Baptist Memorial Hospital in Oxford, MS straight out of nursing school. Initially, I would have a sweet church mother that would allow me to room with her until we could decide our next moves.

We were now attending church at Spirit of Excellence Ministries under the leadership of Bishop Kelvin and Elder Deborah Ransey. Life now consisted of working and attending church in Oxford, so it seemed only logical to live in Oxford. Under this ministry, the Father would begin to plant me. I had learned to encourage myself; he had begun to reveal areas of deliverance in my life, and now it was time to be planted. Destiny was now calling for me to become planted, settled, and steadfast. I would no longer be able to vacillate in the things of God, for now he would begin calling me to maturity in my walk with Christ. With this requirement, there were many experiences that would pull me into the expectations of the Father.

Let me clarify some things before moving forward. In every ministry, God had a plan and had I not walked through every ministry and experience, I would not be who I am today. For that, I appreciate every ministry leader and opportunity that was entrusted to me. I love each of the leaders that have been named; therefore, I would be remiss to write a book and not mention them by name. So much of who I am today, is because of what they have invested in my life. Now, with all being said, let me lay my heart on the next pages of this book!

Through the many years of spiritual and natural struggles the Lord had spoken some noticeably clear things to me. First, through the years of struggling in marriage and the demonic warfare that accompanied this, he said to me, "You must see your husband as a soul." He told me that it would be shameful for me to evangelize everyone else and lose the souls in my home. Now, my husband accepted his call to ministry in 1996 and I accepted my call in 1997. Do not let the acceptance fool you, as we both had many issues to overcome. During these years, as two preachers with issues, we began to come face to face with our hearts and it was ugly encounters all the way around. Yet, we both loved Jesus. We both knew, he alone, was our only way out. Not knowing how we would get there, but knowing if we got there it would be by his grace and mercy.

My husband had been delivered two years prior to our marriage of a drug addiction and dealing with the generational curses and bondages of lust. When we began to confront this demon, I discovered this had been deep rooted in him from a child. As previously stated, at the age of six, he was taught that "if you want a woman, you have to take her." I am grateful the Father showed me his heart before he allowed me to see his issues. There were many times of unfaithfulness, from the church member to the women of the city, and a child born to another woman during our marriage. Yet, my challenge was to see him as a soul. The toughest part is when the soul is intimately and emotionally connected to you. It is easier to labor for souls that do not live in your house, or at least it was for me. It was much easier for me to war for souls that I could leave at the altar and see them the next week at church. But it was quite different when the soul I was assigned to war for slept in the bed with me at night. I want to encourage you, my sister, if this is you – to hang in there.

Now, this may not be every woman's assignment, so I admonish you to pray and know God's direction for your life. I seemed to always be the one who had to forgive, and many times felt as though the unfaithfulness presented me an opportunity to minister to the other woman. I wanted the other woman to know she deserved more. She did not have to be the second, she deserved the first. She did not have to be hidden and covered, she needed to be seen. Then there was the line that had to be drawn in the sand. At what point, would I stop and deal with the inner me? At what point would I allow myself to process the many years of pain, hurt, shame and disappointment. Not only the lust, but then the demonic spirit of jealousy. It was with this spirit of jealousy that the line was drawn. Lust was painful, but jealousy was beyond what I could put into words. What nerves of the devil to commit a marital violation, but then act as though I am covering up something? Jealousy would make him look through my phone log and then question me. I remember a very vivid conversation where I told the devil AND my husband that I would not tolerate this demonic spirit.

The spirit of jealousy degraded me to the lowest degree. It violated my faithfulness to Christ. I was not faithful to my husband because I could not be unfaithful, but I was faithful because I loved my Daddy. So, I begin to verbalize the barriers I would have to cross to be unfaithful. I would have to sneak and arrange a meeting place, then I would have to undress (a married women) and lay in the bed with another man who was not my husband. This man would have intercourse with me, and I would have to find pleasure in the bed with a man that was not mine as a married woman. The thought of this insult violated every yes, I had to God. It was said in that moment, "I have stayed through the lust, but I am not equipped--I will not and cannot stay for the demonic force of jealousy." From that day to this one, I have not dealt with that spirit again! Song of Solomon 8:6 (KJV) declares jealousy is as cruel as the grave and I was not willing to find out!

For me, the Father used these things to work his ultimate plan in my life. It was dealing with the souls in my home that taught me fervency, endurance, perseverance, and trust. It was the first child that made me a mom, that I had fanaticized about loving me unconditionally, that told me to "consider myself dead to him." It was this first child who spent three- and one-half years in a Mississippi prison and during this time, his son had to be cared for. It was also his son's mother that became a child birthed from the soul challenge. When the Lord asked me did I want to take the soul challenge, I passionately cried YES!!! It was this child from the heart that would be in and out of our lives, yet I would have to love her. It was this child that birthed the Jesus Challenge in my life from the last conversation I would have with this child in the confines of my home.

It was the second child, who challenged me not to allow my reputation in church to override my mandate for her soul. It was through an attempted suicide at age 12 that we realized she had been sexually molested since age five. All this was the result of us allowing a family to stay in our home while transitioning from up North to move to Mississippi. Her encounters with molestation occurred weekly after church service and in the home.

It was my third child that taught me how to deal with an irrational demon during his teenage years of rebellion and smoking weed. Yes, it was a lot, but these were real natural life encounters.

Spiritually, I vividly remember when God was ready to extract the "love of church" and inject "the love of him" in my heart. This process was two-and one-half years of very fierce depression. There were days that I could not get out of the bed. There were days the telephone did not ring anymore, and what I once knew had suddenly changed. Why? The thing that had defined who I was in life was being stripped. Church, the love of it, and all things that it entailed had become the definition of who I was as a person. Currently in life, I did not know that salvation was not a birth into a church, but a kingdom. I did not realize God's plan was for me to reproduce kingdom and not church. I did not realize the baptism of the Holy Ghost was for me to establish kingdom culture in the earth. More than servant and Christian, the Father's original intent was for me to become a Son and a citizen.

I remember the day that God delivered me on my living room floor. He told me that I would no longer prove my deliverance, but from that day forth, I would walk in who he called me to be. Did I try to go back to the familiar? Yes! Did I long to be what I once was? Yes! I would ask God often, "What does that look like?" The Father was about to really show me what Destiny displayed really looked like. I was being prepared to "see" some things that I never thought I would "see" in this lifetime on the Earth. None of this transition happened overnight, but these were the years that I could constantly hear the Father saying, "Ready or Not!"

Chapter VI
Destiny Displayed

Into what were you born? This question was rehearsed over and over in my mind. It was the wee hours of the morning on March 19, 2017, I was awakened out of my sleep. The Lord said, "You have been released." At the time, I was unsure as to what all this release entailed. I had a preaching engagement at a local church and this message would certainly coincide with the preached word for the day. As the day progressed, I was to be on a prayer call that night at 9:00 p.m. where the Lord once again confirmed "the release."

During this time, who could imagine the Father would use a book sitting on a table in a church foyer to literally transition the next phase of my life. I had walked past this book for weeks or maybe even months and each time I would sense a need to pay more attention to the book. Finally, one day I picked the book up and brought it home. The book sat in my bedroom for weeks and still no attention. Then, there was the day I could no longer neglect the book. The title was "Rediscovering the Kingdom" by Dr. Myles Monroe. As I picked the book up and began to read the first pages, the Lord said to me, "I am about to uproot religion and download kingdom." He said, "Ty, you can have all of me, but you will have to be willing to travel upstream!" At the time, I did not understand and was certainly apprehensive of the unknown, but with all in my heart it was something I wanted. I desired to know what this looked like. And, for sure, the Father was about to download kingdom at an accelerated pace! Destiny was about to be displayed and I surely had no idea of where this road would lead, but I was willing to follow.

In 2002, I heard the Lord say, "I have called you to Pastor." I remember the reactions I received as I announced this news at the premature time, I heard it. This was all I heard regarding this until the rest of the story began to unfold. From the time I heard this word in 2002 to now 2017, I have gone through many things that did not look like this word. I loved the church and was accustomed to being the church harlot. Though this language could be offensive to some, I want you to allow me to explain. As a matter of fact, it was harsh to me when I realized how many times I played this role in church. Immediately, when we hear the word harlot, we think of a prostitute that has sex for money.

In my case, I had been given gifts that would benefit the church. There were many times my gifts were used for the benefit of someone else and other times abused. The abuse that happens in many churches is more than I wish to bring attention to. As a matter of fact, that is another subject for another book. Many times, church will teach us how to be submissive to leadership without boundaries. Many times, in church there is a tolerance for certain titles that is of a different standard than the "lay members." And the church has a way of justifying these unequivocal standards. Abuse should not be acceptable no matter who it comes from. Whether it is the Pastor the First Lady or the membership to the leaders- abuse is totally unacceptable and the type of abuse is irrelevant. Abuse is abuse. Now, the prostitution of gifts in the church is where I make my point of the church harlot. Prostitution of gifts is the unworthy or corrupt use of one's talent for the sake of personal gain. I was one of the ones who was a victim of this many times.

Many times, I was willing to help in any arena needed. No hidden agendas, simply wanting the leaders to shine. But I lost count of the times the gifts were used and often abused. The times the gifts were used to fulfill personal desires and agendas. The times the gift was used, and it left me standing out in the cold without any defense, uncovered, naked, and ashamed. As we would say, "thrown under the bus." The times the gifts were prostituted in the church. They were used for personal advantage and thrown to the side until needed again. But my testimony is one of triumph! I thank God for every encounter as I would not be who I am today, had I not endured some things in ministry. As stated earlier, severe depression was one ordeal.

I had gone many years being told by the church that I did not know how to talk to people. This proclamation from others had driven me to the prayer floor and begging for God to just help me shut my mouth until I could learn how to talk to others. It was usually the church people who could not identify with the very firm, serious, straight-forward, no non-sense personality the Father created me to be. The intense prayers for the Father to help me shut my mouth continued, until one day the Lord sent a prophet by the name of Pastor Lee Miller to tell me to, "SPEAK!" He emphatically expressed my need to speak for God was about to make all things new in my life. Wow! This was quite different from what I had been praying and asking God for. This was a stark, opposite command. How dare the Lord tell me to speak, when all my life I had been told my ability to speak and to communicate was a dire weakness in my life? Surely, the Lord would not be saying different. I took this word and began to ponder it in my heart. In the pondering, the Lord broke it down like this… He showed me my natural life as a nurse and how I must deal with teams.

At this point in life, I hold a Doctorate of Nursing Practice and this requires a life of communication in various forms. While I will admit I am much greater at written communication than verbal - they both require the skill of communication. There is no way I could be an effective leader in my secular arena IF I did not know how to talk. Nursing had afforded me many leadership roles, and based on professional reviews, communication with others had not been much of an issue. But, when it came to the church arena, communication seemed to be a prominent issue.

It was not until the Father began to uproot religion and download kingdom that all this began to make sense. It was always the plan of the enemy to shut my mouth! For in it were the oracles, governments, and administration of the Kingdom of Heaven. I had been sent by God to "lead, motivate, and inspire others to live from within." I had been "sent by God to establish kingdom order in the Earth." So, if my mouth is shut, there is no way I can fulfill my assignment in the Earth. So, early on the enemy sought to use people to shut my mouth.

With religion very much still a part of my cloth and the release spoken to me in March of 2017, I stepped out to do what I thought I had been called to do. In my religious mind, pastoring certainly was a church building (4 walls), membership and all the other church etiquette that goes along with that. It was a Sunday service, a mid-week service, opening of the doors of the church and all the other religious activity. Now, please do not take that to mean any slight against the church, which was always intended to be the kingdom embassy in the earth. For me, I am simply trying to get to an endpoint. I was ordained a pastor and began doing what I knew, based on my religious experiences, to be pastoring.

It was during this that I knew, without a question, my assignment was to "train soldiers." This assignment was given to me in the 90s, long before I knew any of what was about to happen. When having this conversation as a young woman in the 90s, the prophetic voice of my divine sister, Natoria Kennell-Foster again, spoke to me and said, "If you are going to train soldiers, then you must be a General!" This was just taken to be casual conversation at that time. But here it came to pass, No Longer Bound Outreach Ministries began to meet on Sundays and Tuesdays. Sundays never felt right, they never fit. The wrestle began. I would lay before God and wrestle. Why did Sundays not feel right when you called me to pastor?

There in the wrestle, as I surrendered my flesh to him, he continued to download kingdom. As an enthusiastic pastor, learning kingdom, I would try to PREACH this to all that would listen, until the Father stopped me one day. He said, "Ty, I didn't preach kingdom to the masses!" Wow! Eyes open, mouth shut! He said to me, "When I was ready to TEACH kingdom, I pulled my twelve disciples aside and taught them kingdom." They would go into the world and teach others. He, again, solidified another major part of destiny. He would tell me in the prayer closet, Ty, "If you go, the multitudes will follow." I was lost again. How do I go as a pastor? Leave the sheep and go? Then he would, on multiple occasions say to me, "Don't try to explain my call and assignment on your life. You train the soldiers, and they will go to their respective places and teach kingdom."

Then, in the early months of 2018, the moment came that solidified and totally rearranged the initial structure of ministry for me. One night I was praying, repenting, and asking God the next steps. I had realized that all I knew was the picture of pastoring that had been presented and my religious mind tried to display his word in my life. I began to ask him what he meant by go and being sent when the call of pastoring consisted of sheep. He simply reiterated the rest of the statement from 2002! He said, "I called you to pastor the pastors and shepherd the shepherds!" This date with destiny answered every question while presenting even greater challenges to my yet, transforming religious mind.

The Lord began to deal with me deeper in the call. I am entering the fourth year of No Longer Bound Outreach Ministry and the Lord continues to display destiny in my life. He has taken me underground to free slaves and train soldiers. This is my assignment in the Earth. He has taken me back to the book "Rediscovering the Kingdom" and told me this time will be an even deeper revelation of the kingdom in my life. The journey continues and transformation of my mind continues daily. The flesh is being crucified and God's destiny is continuing to unfold in my life. The enemy expected me to fail, but God destined for me to succeed!

Conclusion

One must view life from the proper kingdom perspective. The enemy's perspective can always show you the opportunities for victimization and promotes a Babylonian system that will assist you in remaining the victim. The Father's Kingdom always intended for us to be victorious and has provided us with every means necessary to walk in victory. We must have the correct kingdom response. The world's response will always be undergirded in the lust of the eyes, lust of the flesh, and the pride of life. On the other hand, the Kingdom of Heaven's response will always cause you to rejoice in every opportunity to expand the kingdom. We are in an awesome time of kingdom innovation during this pandemic.

Destiny has not stopped its courtship because of the current pandemic, neither has our Father stopped being Abba; Jesus being the Christ, or Holy Spirit the power that yet quickens our mortal man. We must gird up the loins of our mind and know that we will overcome the enemy by the blood of the lamb and the words of our testimony loving not our lives unto the death (Revelation 12:11KJV).

As a child without much remembrance of childhood, a teenage mother, high school dropout; a saved but undelivered saint, religious at best - I thank God for loving me enough to reveal kingdom to me. From the beginning, Satan expected me to fail. In hopes of promoting his plan he surrounded me with a troubled, abusive older brother, a baby at 15, a husband bound by generational bondages, religion over relationship, and many half-directed moves in my spiritual walk thus far. Without a doubt, Satan's expectation was always for me to fail.

Abba, my heavenly Father, before the foundation of the world, destined me to succeed. In his infinite wisdom and love for me he sent his son Jesus to die a horrible, undeserved death, to restore the kingdom to me! Jesus chose me when others never saw me. He, in eternity, stepped into time and walked out my end from the beginning. He then placed me in time to fulfill everything he ordained me to be. He knew during the abusive relationship with my brother that this would be needed to produce the warrior mentality I would desperately need to fight. He knew with the baby at 15, I would need to be able to minister life after the fall to others who would come after me. He knew the marriage would look a mess to the world, but would produce a testimony of a heart that understands true forgiveness. He allowed me to experience the womb of church because he knew he would birth me into the revelation truth of the kingdom. As the prophet Ezekiel in Ezekiel 3:15 (KJV), he has allowed me to sit where people have sat, because he knew I would need these experiences for ministry. He placed people in my path that would impact my life along the way, because he knew I would be required to live the same life. He blessed me with a husband who had a heart for him and issues for he knew someone would need to be able to talk about a God who could change a marriage mess into a miracle.

It was in marriage I learned true love. I learned that God loved me despite myself. How? I have a husband that convinced me that he loved me. Had I never experienced church and religion I would have never longed for kingdom and relationship. Had I never known the experiences of being the church harlot, I would have never been able to appreciate those who really love you without any strings attached. I am the warrior and servant I am today because I had an enemy that expected me to fail, but a God that destined me to succeed.

Listen, we must be careful of how we see things in life. It is the job of the adversary (Satan) to make you see things from the wrong perspective. We must employ our afflictions and make them work for us! According to 2 Corinthians 4:17- our light affliction, which is but for a moment, worketh for us a far more exceeding and eternal weight of glory…as a believer, we must understand that affliction came to work for us. Allow this current affliction to reveal the exceeding and eternal weight of glory that God intended. We all have a story. I remember praying to the Father and telling him, "I don't mind going through IF someone will be helped by this trial." Today, I am humbled to see the afflictions working for me! I am humbled to know that I may not can meet you face to face to share the story, but prayerfully, the words on these pages will cause you to see life in a different perspective. The depression, the thoughts of suicide, the teenage pregnancy, the times of no income, no food, no celebrations because of no money, the heartaches, and the pain - IT all was working in me for a greater glory. Your dark hours may not feel like you are gaining anything, and it may seem that morning will never come! I understand, I have seen these days. Honestly, I still see these days. There are still days that I have soul wounds reopened and they begin to bleed all over again. Places in my heart, I thought was healed, only to discover they are still healing and there remains some raw places. I want to encourage you to believe and know; destiny is being fulfilled in your life. I want you to believe and know that Jesus died for you! He died for you to experience freedom in the earth. He died for you to live life and not just life but ABUNDANT life! There are some things I am assured of and you must be also. One is God is for me! He loved you so much he sent his son to die for you with "no strings attached."

This became revelation for me in 2015 after I was privileged to donate a kidney. After the kidney donation, a banquet was being hosted for the donor and the recipient to be celebrated. My recipient and his family were going through some transitions and he did not attend. I was hurt for a moment! First, the Lord asked me if I wanted to be a part of HIS miracle. My answer was yes to HIS miracle. So, what right did I have to be angry during this banquet? Obviously, none! As the Lord ministered to me one morning, while driving to work, he began to show me how he died for the world and his expectation is for us to accept his invitation to salvation. Yet, many of us never show up, but he yet loves us, and it is with "no strings attached!" He said, "I allowed you to participate in someone else's miracle and there were no strings attached!" May YOU the reader understand this - The devil EXPECTS YOU TO FAIL, BUT YOUR HEAVENLY FATHER ALWAYS DESTINED YOU TO SUCCEED!!!

In closing, I want to share that I suffered yet another life altering experience during writing this book. On August 31, 2020 I was released to close my medical practice. This was the second time in life that I have felt and processed the depths of grief. I will go to the grave or be raptured knowing that in September 2016, the manifestation of the vision for a medical practice given to me while driving down the road was set in motion. The doors of this practice opened for business on January 9, 2017. For three and one-half years I trusted God with ALL of me to maintain what he started. I remember Daddy calling the workers by name to be employed at the practice. I remember having to meet payroll and laying in the floor reminding God how he called the employees there and it was his business to provide for their salaries. Not one time did I miss payroll, and it was always on time. This is a testament to the God I serve. It was in the medical practice that God gave me a platform to minister to the whole man.

I literally witnessed the cases who came to the clinic just in the nick of time for their lives to be spared. God allowed me to minister to pastors and pastor's wives, and ministry leaders in their place of brokenness and I witnessed their restoration by the power of God. It was in this space that my life seemed complete. Yet, three and one-half years later, Daddy released me with an urgency. My last clinic was on July 30, 2020, he had already assigned me to pray the month of August 2020, and I was to be out of the clinic before September 2020. The clinic was officially closed on August 31, 2020. To many it would seem the clinic had succumbed to the pandemic. And while my professional response would not correct this thinking, the spiritual man always knew the Father had snatched me out of the medical arena. In the place of turmoil, a distraught heart, and overwhelming grief as I had to let go of people who has trusted me to care for them, I had to sit in the face of hundreds of patients and tell them I was closing.

For weeks, I sobbed with them and my heart ached as I told them I would be closing my doors and they would have to establish care elsewhere. I am hard wired to care and there was no way I could walk away without a face to face with each patient. I felt like I owed them a conversation, although it would not change the outcome. There I was, my heart exposed and vulnerable while doing the only thing I knew to do, which was to cry, pray, and trust Daddy. Again, I am at a place in life where destiny is yet being fulfilled. During an extremely low day, Daddy had me on the heart of one of his Apostolic generals. I would receive a phone call from Apostle Linda Rogers…you know the one who I first met at the Baptist Church, yes, she would call to simply tell me, "Don't lose this assignment!" I see the hand of Daddy doing so much in my life. I can see some things clearly regarding where we are. I yet see the enemy's plan for failure in my life, but I have matured to know that because Daddy destined me to succeed - it is a done deal. The fight is fixed!! WE WIN!!

www.ingramcontent.com/pod-product-compliance
Lightning Source LLC
Chambersburg PA
CBHW071141090426
42736CB00012B/2195